Can Meditation Be Done?

Conscious Union With God

Thomas Hora, M.D.

The PAGL Foundation, Inc.
New York, New York

1999
The PAGL Foundation, Inc.

Copyright © 1985 by Thomas Hora, M.D.

All rights reserved. No part of this book may be reproduced, stored in a retrieval system or transmitted, in any form or by any means electronic, mechanical, photocopying, recording or otherwise, without the written permission of the PAGL Foundation, Inc.

Printed in the United States of America

ISBN 0-913105-09-0

ISBN series 0-913105-01-5

The PAGL Foundation, Inc.
New York, New York

TABLE OF CONTENTS

Meditation 1
Imagination and Visualization 5
Finding Our Soul 8
The Living Soul 9
Visualization Versus Realization 11
The Firmament 13
Beholding 14
Transitional Struggle 16
Thinking and Awareness 17
The Buddha Versus The Thinker 19
The Two Shall Be One 21
Three Levels of Meditation 21
The Bible and Meditation 23
The Prayer of Right Seeing 24
Prayer as a Mental Health Principle 25
The Prayer of Beholding 27
Meditation on the Lord's Prayer 30
The Four W's 31
The Prayer of Glowing 32
Two Meditations 32

INTRODUCTION

Thomas Hora, M.D., (1914-1995), was a psychiatrist with a passion for seeking spiritual understanding. His search led him to study philosophy as well as psychology, and the wisdom of world religions. Most important to him were the spiritual teachings of Jesus Christ, which became the cornerstone of his practice which he called Metapsychiatry. Metapsychiatry offers a unique method of healing which blends psychological insights with metaphysical truths about who and what we really are.

The appeal of Metapsychiatry is broad and deep and transcends denominations. Dr. Hora's patients and students included Catholics, Protestants, Jews, Buddhists, and non-religious individuals. Some of these individuals went on to become counselors and teachers themselves.

From 1983 to 1987 a group of them* led by Jan Linthorst, D. Min., distilled the essence of his wisdom on 12 vital subjects and published them as a series of booklets. This is one of them. The others, as well as books and tapes of Dr. Hora, are available through the PAGL Foundation. PAGL is an acronym for Peace, Assurance, Gratitude, and

Love, qualities of being which are accompanied by blessings and healings. The presence of PAGL in consciousness, Dr. Hora taught, is evidence of the existence of God and can be seen as a way by which to measure individual spiritual progress.

Dr. Hora's genius was first to help individuals see their problems in terms of invalid values, beliefs and modes of living, and them to help them to see their lives in the context of God and to learn to replace troublesome, unhealthy values with valid ones. Only then, he taught, could problems dissolve and PAGL take their place. Each booklet in this series gives a different glimpse of this process.

*Ann Linthorst, Joan Taylor, Joan Rubadeau and Gloria Spurgeon

MEDITATION

A little boy was weeding a strawberry patch. A man passing by said, "This is amazing. There are so many kinds of weeds. How do you know which ones to pull out?" The little boy answered: "Mister, I only know the strawberries!" So it is with meditation. There are so many theories and practices, one could get dizzy trying to study them all.

The most frequently asked question is: How do you meditate? This is a futile question. It is a peculiarity of the personal mind to be naturally hypocritical and operational. It is hypocritical because it pretends to know what meditation is, and it is operational because it assumes that it can be "done." The result of this is that multitudes of so-called seekers after the truth are performing certain ritualistic techniques of meditation without having the slightest idea of what to expect or what the issue is. This is an exercise in futility and self-deception. The sixth principle of Metapsychiatry is: "If you know *what*, you know *how*." Anyone who knows what meditation is will know how to meditate.

Therefore, let us ask first, What is meditation? Meditation is a wholehearted attentiveness to what God wants. Second, What is the right motivation for meditation? The right motivation for meditation is a sincere interest in committing oneself to being here for God. Most people, however, approach the issue of meditation with the idea of getting something for themselves. They seek to get something out of it. This sounds very sensible. Man assumes that God is here to satisfy his personal desires. Unfortunately, this is not so. God is not a servant of man—man is an image and likeness of God. God is not interested in what we want. God is interested in what He wants. In Metapsychiatry, we meditate for God. Does God need our meditation? Yes. God created man to manifest His qualities in the world. Meditation is a way of recommitting oneself to that task.

Everything in the universe has a built-in intentionality. Flowers and trees seem to have the intention to manifest the glory of their essential nature to the fullest extent. This intentionality can be discerned in everything in God's universe.

In meditation we focus our attention on the will of God so that we might come into ever more perfect alignment with the built-in intentionality of the creative Principle — God. Thus we are learning to be here for God and not for ourselves, or for someone else. Anyone who understands this cannot possibly ask anymore how to meditate. God has created us for himself that we may show forth His glory, and we are here for that purpose.

The human race seems to be cursed with an ability to be distracted and to ignore the will of God. This ability is called self-confirmatory ideation. Meditation is not an activity — it is an action of the soul. The Virgin Mary said: "My soul doth magnify the Lord" (Luke 1:46). The soul is responsive to the intentionality of creation. When we have learned to be what God has meant us to be, then our lives are most harmonious, efficient, effortless, and effective.

The Bible describes the effects of meditation the following way: "Prepare ye the way of the Lord, make straight in the desert a highway for our God. Every valley shall be exalted, and every mountain and hill shall be made low and the crooked shall be made straight, and the rough places plain" (Isaiah 40:4,5). This means that meditation opens our awareness to the reality and nature of God and this, in turn, has its beneficial consequences: the barreness of ignorant life gives way to fruitfulness; the mountains of self-aggrandizement are brought down; the valleys of self-depreciation are elevated to levels of health, the crooked mentalities become honest and forthright, and abrasive personalities become frictionless. If we learn to be here for God, then our mode of being-in-the-world becomes harmonious, egoless, frictionless and fruitful.

In meditation we become conscious of the fact that our being is an aspect of infinite Being. We gain a broad perspective on Reality and our participation in this Reality. The universal tendency of unenlightened man is to slide into ever narrower perspectives. There is a tendency to become narrow-minded and to suffer the consequences. For instance, a young mother who was scheduled to address a PTA meeting, developed a sore throat and became hoarse. In examining the symptom, we discovered that she imagined that she would bring her throat to that meeting and her throat would have to deliver her speech. In other words, her mental horizon had narrowed down to an organ of her body. When she considered the fact that the members of the PTA expected to meet the totality of her being — which is an expression of God's being — her throat cleared up.

In connection with the issue of narrow-mindedness, there is a story about a young medical student who came home for vacation and paid a visit to the local family doctor. When the doctor asked him about his studies, the medical student said proudly: "I am not going to be a general practitioner, but a specialist. I have decided to specialize in diseases of the nose." The old doctor remained quiet for a while; then he asked with great sincerity, 'And which nostril?"

IMAGINATION AND VISUALIZATION

There is much controversy about the role of imagination, visualization and fantasy in connection with meditation. There is a widespread belief that the creative process, and even healing work, entails the application of these faculties of the human mind. In the Bible there seems to be no indication that God engages in imaginations, fantasies or visualizations. It appears that God creates by proclamation. "Let there be light" (Genesis 1:3). "Let there be a firmament" (Genesis 1:6). God cannot possibly use imagination because God is not a creator of forms. God creates nondimensional realities. Now the question is: Who creates forms? Forms are not created. They are phenomena, or appearances. They are thoughts in visible form. Imaginations and fantasies are activities of an illusory mind engaged in creating forms. The counterfeit mind is engaged in producing a counterfeit reality. The Bible says that God has created us in His own image and likeness (Genesis 1:26). To understand this intriguing statement, we must ask, What is the image of nondimensional Being and what is His likeness? What does God look like? And what do we look like in the eyes of God? God creates Living Souls. What is the shape of a Living Soul? A Living Soul is never born and never dies and is "hid with Christ in God" (Colossians 3:3).

Lately, there is a growing tendency by some doctors and so-called holistic healers to recommend the use of imagination, fantasy and so-called visualization techniques in the treatment of diseases and pursuits of ambitions. The idea is that whatever one wants and visualizes will happen. It is a way of telling God what we want and He will give it to us. "Ask, and it shall be given you" (Matt. 7:7, Luke 11:9), especially if you ask it in Jesus' name. The amazing thing is that this occasionally seems to work. What happens when a sickness is healed on the basis of imagination? The answer is, we have a case of imaginary health. In what way is imaginary health different from real health?

In order to understand this we must first consider the nature of imagination and fantasy.

To imagine something means to give form to an idea which is formless. Forms are dimensional. With the help of imagination, we are moving into the world of dimensionality which consists of one, two, or three-dimensional objects. A famous Zen koan says: "Form is formlessness and formlessness is form," which indicates that in the phenomenal world there is constant interplay between various dimensional appearances.

One of the most famous literary figures, Dr. Faustus, is described by Goethe as a brilliant scholar who kept visualizing himself as the most outstanding and powerful scientist in the world. One day a personage appeared before him who offered him the fulfillment of his fantasies for a price. Namely, the loss of his soul. "What shall it profit a man, if he shall gain the whole world, and lose his own soul?" (Mark 8:36). We can get anything we want for the price of our soul. We lose our sense of spiritual identity and become power-mad. Psychiatrists have known for a long time that insanity is a belief in the power and reality of personal fantasies and imaginations. When fantasy is perceived as reality, we are insane.

Reality is spiritual, therefore it is neither form nor formlessness — it is nondimensional. If we resort to visualizations, imaginations and fantasies as prayer and worshiping, we are unwittingly inviting the devil (personal mind) to sign a contract with him. The second commandment warns us against image-making. Notwithstanding, the human race cherishes the faculty of imagination. Children are encouraged to use their imaginations, we speak of creative imagination, etc. Real artistic creativity, however, is based on inspired ideas reaching the artist's consciousness from the divine Mind.

But when imagination and visualization become a religious ritual, we are in trouble, because then we are entering an illusory world of our own creating. Whatever we can imagine remains purely imaginary, even if it seems to be a healing. In contradistinction to imaginary healings where we gain the world and lose our soul, real healing happens when we find our soul and lose the world.

FINDING OUR SOUL

What do we mean by finding our soul and losing the world? The Bible says, "Love not the world, neither the things that are in the world. If any man love the world, the love of the Father is not in him" (1 John 2:15). Real healing then consists of finding the soul. How do we find our soul? What happens when we are beginning to see that we are Living Souls? How can we understand the fact that by finding our souls we can be healed of whatever ails us? This question is answered by the tenth principle of Metapsychiatry, which says: "The understanding of what really is, abolishes all that seems to be."

The great question remains, How can we become aware of ourselves as Living Souls? The soul cannot be imagined. We cannot draw a picture of it. We cannot visualize it because it is nondimensional. The nondimensional can, however, be "beheld." What is beholding? Beholding is seeing with our faculty of spiritual discernment or the inner eye or, as the Oriental sages speak of it, with the third eye. This faculty can be awakened in us by learning to "look not upon the things which are seen, but at the things which are not seen: for the things which are seen are temporal (unreal); but the things that are not seen are eternal (real)" (2 Corinthians 4:18).

THE LIVING SOUL

In Metapsychiatry, "soul" is a word used to describe a nondimensional entity which is alive, which was never born, and which never dies. It is synonymous with the Christ. It is a quality of consciousness attained through the process of studying and meditating on ultimate issues. When we realize that we are Living Souls, we have beheld ourselves in the context of God. The Buddhists speak about the Buddha nature. Both these concepts point to the Christ consciousness.

The aim of Zen training is to realize one's own Buddha nature. The aim of metapsychiatric study is to realize oneself as a Living Soul which was never born and never dies, which is "hid with Christ in God," and which is the source of everything real and good and beautiful. All the qualities and ideas flow from God into this individual Living Soul, which we all are. When we say that everything and everyone is here for God, we mean that we are Living Souls at different levels of realization. When Buddhists speak of the "unborn," it is the same thing as the Living Soul, the ultimate nondimensional entity which is the true identity for everyone.

This reminds us of the Zen master who asks: "Show me your face which you had before your parents were born." This koan liberates us from the fantasies of our parents. We have often spoken about the fact that we are unconsciously living out the fantasies of our parents. Now, the koan says we have to realize our true identities, which are completely antecedent to any parental fantasies about us. In order to really be aware of one's true identity, one has to be free from parental and educational influences. In working with this koan, one can reach a point of total freedom from other people's thoughts. Buddha said that we are what we think, having become what we have thought (and we must add, under the influence of others). Therefore, we seek liberation by becoming aware of ourselves as God has created us. This process of liberation is the freedom to be what God wants us to be. Our spiritual selfhood is "hid with Christ in God." It is hidden from ourselves and from the world because few suspect it. Few can really understand it. It is a mysterious sense of identity beyond the comprehension of unenlightened man. It cannot be apprehended by the senses, but we can come to know it through the spiritual faculty of beholding. The beholder beholds his own true identity, which is devoid of all human influences. This is complete authenticity of being.

VISUALIZATION VERSUS REALIZATION

It is not advisable to attempt to visualize a Living Soul. If we are eager to form images in our consciousness, it means we are descending into the dimensional world, and we don't really understand ourselves as Living Souls. We just imagine things. Whatever we can imagine will be purely imaginary. We will not be aware of Reality but only of fantasies. It is to escape from fantasies that we have to realize nondimensional Reality. The Living Soul is pure wisdom and love and individualized spiritual life. It cannot be visualized, and we cannot draw a picture of it. If we try, we lose it. We cannot even think about it. We have to be aware of ourselves as nondimensional units of awareness. God is infinite Mind. Infinity has no dimensions. We cannot measure infinity; it is nondimensional, and everything in the context of infinite Mind is also nondimensional. The human mind cannot conceive of anything nondimensional. The human mind is an illusion anyway. God is the Mind which makes it possible to be aware of Reality. Whatever can be imagined cannot be real. It is easy to kid ourselves that we are in touch with Reality when trying to visualize it.

When we speak of material man, we speak of the phenomenal world. In this world, everything is an illusion. Even seeing man as a dimensional form is illusion. When we ask, What sees man? we can only say, the so-called carnal mind sees dimensional reality. Dimensional reality could be thought of as a dream or a shadow. In order to be liberated from the problems of the phenomenal world, we have to reach a realization of nondimensional Reality, which is unimaginable, but discernible spiritually.

THE FIRMAMENT

In the Bible, God said: "Let there be a firmament, and let us divide the waters which are below the firmament from the waters which are above the firmament" (Genesis 1:6-7). Metapsychiatry interprets this as saying: The waters below the firmament are the "sea of mental garbage" in which unenlightened man lives and struggles, appears to be born, gets sick and dies. This is what seems to be going on below the firmament. The firmament itself we understand to be the faculty of awareness, which we call spiritual discernment. This faculty makes it possible to be aware of the difference between the phenomenal world and noumenal Reality. Above the firmament is the infinite "ocean of Love-Intelligence." The firmament is the dividing line which is not structural, but a faculty of awareness. Until this faculty is awakened in us, we don't know spiritual Reality. All we know is the "sea of mental garbage." When we start studying Metapsychiatry, we discover that there are other dimensions to life, and then we gradually awake to the faculty of awareness, spiritual discernment. The word "discernment" refers to a capacity to separate Reality from unreality. It is like separating the tares from the wheat, as Jesus describes in his parable (Matthew 13:24-30). When a farmer's workers discovered tares in the field of wheat, they came to him and asked, "What shall we do? The whole field is infested with this poisonous weed and everything is lost." The farmer said, "Wait until harvest time. When the wheat becomes ripe, then you will be able to discern the difference between the tares and the wheat and you will separate the two." When we reach the harvest time of our spiritual development, then the faculty of discernment emerges in consciousness, and we have the ability to separate Reality from unreality. The spiritual and the material can now be clearly seen, and that constitutes the emergence of the firmament. From here on, we are working and praying and meditating in the direction of rising ever higher, to the point of beholding.

BEHOLDING

Beyond the firmament is the faculty of beholding. This beholding is the capacity to see spiritual Reality. At this point we may discover that we are Living Souls, incorporeal, nondimensional spiritual identities, living in the context of infinite Mind. We are not dealing any more with images but with realizations of our individual places in that Reality. Interestingly enough, at that point our lives begin to improve in every direction. We are harvesting the blessings of expanded awareness, of spiritual consciousness. Our understanding of ourselves as Living Souls becomes evident in healings in our bodies, in our so-called temperament, and in our relationships to the world. Experiences become more harmonious. We find ourselves responding to daily challenges in more intelligent and effective ways. There is less strain in living, increasing effectiveness, and new blessings.

The material world is seen as the shadow of Reality, a shadow of true substance. In proportion that we are aware of the perfection of life in the nondimensional realm, the shadow images cease to torment us; they disappear because there is nothing to feed them. A Living Soul is unhampered by inanities, the fantasies, the wants and not-wants of the world; therefore, Love-Intelligence can freely express itself in life. As a result, things are less complicated; there is less stress. Whatever is needed is responded to effortlessly, efficiently and effectively.

TRANSITIONAL STRUGGLE

Before the harvest time there is often a period of war between the spirit and the flesh. It is a conflict of interests. If there is conflict within us, it means that we have not yet reached a wholehearted interest in the spiritual life. We are just straddling the firmament, so to speak. That is where the flesh wars against the spirit. The soul does not enter into issues below the firmament. The firmament, being the dividing line between the "sea of mental garbage" and the "ocean of Love-Intelligence," is aware of both so-called worlds. The firmament is awareness. The firmament knows whether we live under the firmament or whether we sincerely seek to rise above it. Most of the struggle consists in turning away from ego-gratification. Ego-gratification is what drives the unenlightened world. Everything that is accomplished by unenlightened man is accomplished in quest of ego-gratification. Enlightened man is an instrument of omniactive Love-Intelligence, the creative Principle of the universe.

THINKING AND AWARENESS

Question: If I am seeing a flower, am I aware of the flower or am I just thinking about seeing a flower? What is the difference between thinking and awareness?

In response to this question, two examples come to mind. The first one is about a British military man who went to India to study with a guru. After several years of intensive work in meditation, he had a very strange experience which he described in a book entitled *On Having No Head*, by D. E. Harding. In this book the author relates that one day, while walking on a crowded street in Bombay, he suddenly had a surprising realization that he did not have a head. Strangely enough, this did not frighten him. On the contrary, it gave him a great sense of peace, assurance, and freedom. With this realization came a heightened sense of awareness of his surroundings, an ability to appreciate beauty, goodness, and truth, and to respond to all things intelligently and with compassion.

The second example is that of a mother who came to consult a psychiatrist upon recommendation of school authorities, who were unable to cope with her two children. These children were bright and knowledgeable but out of control, hyperactive, argumentative, contentious, and disruptive in the classroom. They had a seemingly irresistible urge to prove that they were smarter than their teachers, yet their tests were mostly unsatisfactory.

In exploring the mother's mode of being-in-the-world, it became clear that the mother entertained a secret belief that all intelligence comes from the head and that she was a proud possessor of a particularly good head. She was in the habit of encouraging her children to "use their heads" to figure things out for themselves, to think a lot and to be very smart.

So here we have a man who goes to India and becomes liberated by "losing his head," and on the other side we see a woman who cherishes her head and produces two sick children. What conclusions can we draw from these two examples? It would seem that awareness is health-promoting and thinking is illness-producing. The question may be asked, What makes thinking illness-producing? First of all, we can clearly see that thinking is self-confirmatory. The thinker is inclined to take credit for his thoughts and be either proud of them or ashamed of them.

THE BUDDHA VERSUS THE THINKER

One of the fundamental insights of Metapsychiatry is that self-confirmatory ideation is a common denominator in all human problems. It is a remarkable fact that the sculptor Rodin conceived his famous statue "The Thinker" as the centerpiece of his great work, "The Gate of Hell." Apparently, he was inspired by the same insight as Metapsychiatry about the invalidity and futility of the illusion that man can produce thoughts in his head. Elsewhere we have drawn a comparison between Rodin's "The Thinker" and statues of the Buddha. "The Thinker" depicts a tormented human figure, and the Buddha is a serenely majestic model of infinite awareness and compassion.

Man is tormented by the illusion that he can produce thoughts in his head. Enlightened man has discovered that he is *aware* of thoughts which obtain in consciousness. Man is an individualized unit of awareness. The question is, Can awareness be done? No. Then who is it that is aware? And where is awareness located? What is the organ of awareness? The Zen masters say, "Awareness is aware. The thinker and the thought are one. The dreamer and the dream are one."

The Bible speaks of the soul. Man is a Living Soul. We are hid with Christ in God. It is the soul which has the faculty of spiritual awareness and discernment. Man is a spiritual being. He is an individualized aspect of infinite divine Mind, the creative intelligence underlying all nondimensional reality.

So now we are faced with a surprising paradox: to have a "good head on your shoulders" is insanity, and to have no head at all is glorious liberty. Unenlightened man longs to have personal mind-power with which to control others and secure his own position in life. Enlightened man sees himself as an emanation of divine Mind reflecting the Christ, the "Buddha nature," the qualities of God. Metapsychiatry speaks of man as a nondimensional unit of awareness. The center of all power, perception, comprehension, creative intelligence, is the divine Mind in which we "live and move and have our being" (Acts 17:28).

A famous Zen koan says, "Enlightened man sees with his ears and hears with his eyes." This koan apparently aims at shaking the foundation of the belief in what seems so self-evident to the senses.

THE TWO SHALL BE ONE

In the Gospel according to Thomas, Jesus is quoted as saying: "The Kingdom of God shall come when the inside will be outside and the outside inside, and the two shall be one, and the male with the female, neither male nor female." In the context of our present consideration, we may understand him as saying: "Enlightenment reveals that the outside world of visible forms is an externalization of internal thoughts which are formless. Therefore, 'form is formlessness and formlessness is form.'" The two are actually one. The male sex and the female sex are externalized forms of male and female qualities which are formless. Gender is externalized as sex. Sex is form, gender is quality. Enlightened man is neither male nor female. He is one Living Soul, a nondimensional unit of awareness endowed with all the qualities of God.

THREE LEVELS OF MEDITATION

There are several levels of meditation. There is *contemplative meditation,* where we are seeking clarity on a certain biblical passage or on a principle. We take a principle and seek to understand it, we contemplate the meaning of the words and the relevancy of that principle to our life experience. Meditation on being here for God could be called *existential meditation*. One seeks to realize being here for God and so improve one's mode of being-in-the world. Then the highest form of meditation could be called *spiritual meditation*. Here we are seeking to realize the Living Soul, which was never born and never dies and is hid with Christ in God. To realize the Living Soul is the highest form of meditation because it is synonymous with enlightenment. The essence of all spiritual study and growth is the abolishing of the illusion of existence apart from God. Now when it comes to this highest form of meditation, it cannot be practiced until one has reached a readiness for it. We have to always start at the beginning. So we begin by contemplative meditation of biblical passages, metapsychiatric principles and teachings. We contemplate their relevancy to our daily life and experiences. From there we go to the existential meditation, where our mode of being is the issue. We learn to be here for God. This is the place where healing takes place — physical, emotional, economic, and social. After we have learned to be here for God, we progress naturally into spiritual meditation where the aim is no longer healing, but enlightenment.

We move from verbal prayer to contemplative meditation, to nonverbal awareness of inspired ideas continuously flowing into consciousness from an infinite source. The ideas which flow into such a receptive consciousness are always relevant to the need of the moment even though they may seem "far out." God's ideas seem to us far out — meaning strangely irrelevant — and yet they are supremely relevant.

THE BIBLE AND MEDITATION

Is there instruction in the Bible as to meditation? Some may think of meditation as non-Christian because the Old and New Testaments say relatively little about it. The Buddhists and Taoists speak of it a great deal. But there are references in the Bible to meditation. "Be still and know that I am God" (Psalm 46:10). "Blessed is the man . . . that delighteth in the law of the Lord; and in his law does he meditate day and night" (Psalm 1:1,2). "I will meditate in thy statutes" (Psalm 119:48). "Let the words of my mouth, and the meditation of my heart, be acceptable in they sight, O Lord, my strength, and my redeemer" (Psalm 19:14). "My mouth shall speak of wisdom; and the meditation of my heart shall be of understanding" (Psalm 49:3). "My meditation of Him shall be sweet: I will be glad in the Lord" (Psalm 104:34). "O how love I thy law! It is my meditation all the day" (Psalm 119:97). "Thy testimonies are my meditation" (Psalm 119:99).

In meditation we become very still. Even our thought processes stop. In that stillness we become aware that God is the only source of life, intelligence, love, power, and healing. So meditation is learning to be still in order to realize God is the only "I am." God is the only Ego.

THE PRAYER OF RIGHT SEEING

There is a way of increasing our receptivity to divine impartations and in Metapsychiatry it is called meditating on "right seeing," which is included in the "seven steps of seeing" (see Discourse entitled "Forgiveness.") On the seventh level is beholding. How do we get to that level? A good way is to meditate daily to understand that everything and everyone in the entire universe is here for God, whether they know it or not. That includes ourselves, of course. We will find that the more we contemplate this reality, the more we see things in the context of infinity. That is of great value, because our ideas depend on the perspective with which we view life. Intelligent ideas come to us when our perspective is on infinity. Practicing the prayer of right seeing will increase our capacity to behold all things in the context of infinite Mind.

PRAYER AS A MENTAL HEALTH PRINCIPLE

In meditation we can rise above fantasies and the pollutants of daily impressions. At night we purify our consciousness from the pollutants of the day, and in the morning we clean our consciousness from the pollutants of the night. We do this by turning our attention to spiritual values. We become aware of what is valid and what is not valid and we are separating ourselves from it. The garbage thoughts are not our thoughts. They are just garbage. If there is dust in our living room, it is not our dust. It is just dust. We clean it up, but if we become possessive of our dust, we may accumulate a lot of it. It is not possible to empty our minds because it would take an ego to get rid of the ego. The content of our mind actually constitutes the ego. If we wanted to empty our minds, we would have to resort to a second ego to get rid of the first ego, but then we would still have an ego. So all meditations which endeavor to achieve emptiness through sheer will, or through some kind of technique of breathing or counting, etc., do not really succeed. Fortunately, there are aspects of Reality which are unimaginable — for instance spiritual values. We cannot form images of spiritual values, ideas and qualities. We value highly Love-Intelligence as a synonym for God. Nobody can form an image in his mind of Love-Intelligence. Therefore, by focusing our attention on Love-Intelligence as an existential manifestation, we find that all imagery disappears from consciousness. That way we attain a certain emptiness. The Zen Buddhists speak of "emptiness," which means being free of calculative thoughts, fantasies, concepts, and reaching a state of peaceful consciousness.

There is a story about a student of Zen, who in the course of meditation reached a point where she spontaneously exclaimed, "The bottom of the bucket has broken through!" We understand this to mean that this individual had suddenly become aware of the fact that all mental content had left her and that she had become completely available to inspired wisdom reaching her from the cosmic Mind. If we have a bucket and if we knock out the bottom, what will we get? We get a funnel. A funnel is something that lets everything through and doesn't hold on to anything. We cannot accumulate knowledge, information, fantasies, or imaginings in a funnel. So unenlightened man's consciousness could be compared to a bucket which is constantly being replenished, kept full of images, concepts and preconceived ideas. Enlightened man lets go of these things and as a result, he becomes an open funnel or a channel through which inspired wisdom — Love-Intelligence — freely flows. Such an individual is spontaneously wise, loving and responsive and always capable of dealing with life in an appropriate fashion.

THE PRAYER OF BEHOLDING

Beholding is the highest level of awareness. It is God's presence clearly discerned. It is not something we "do." It is something we develop a capability for. It is happening to us by the grace of God. First, there is the faculty of focusing attention. We have this God-given faculty. This may be the essence of what the Bible describes as "dominion." "And God gave man dominion over the fish of the sea, and over the fowl of the air, and over the cattle, and over all the earth, and over every creeping thing that creepeth upon the earth" (Gen. 1:26). We have dominion over God's creations, and we can focus our attention from one thing to another and also on divine Reality. When our spiritual faculties have expanded to an optimum level, beholding takes place. It is a participation in God's perfect creation. A conscious awareness of God's perfection erases all imperfections. It reveals itself to us as a healing. When Jesus healed a leper, he may have beheld the purity of God's perfect creation. He was able to see this leper in the light of truth. This resulted in healing. The leper could see himself through the eyes of Jesus.

There is another point here. If our intention is to heal someone, then we assume an operational position. We may want to heal another person. But we cannot heal. Only God heals. God is truth. However, beholding an individual in the context of the truth can have an effect of spiritual blessedness. What does it mean to behold someone in the context of truth? It is helpful to remember that everyone is a place where God's presence reveals itself as omniactive Love-Intelligence. Everything in this universe is here for the purpose of manifesting the qualities of God. If we behold others as places where God expresses His own nature, then we lose sight of the human person — of personality quirks, distortions of character, or worried individuals. All we see are the qualities of God manifesting themselves in a certain individual. The primary issue is not to produce a healing, but a willingness to behold the presence of God right where a worried or frightened or sick individual seems to be.

We must be careful not to be self-righteous about meditative practice. We must not turn it into an ego trip. "The fear of the Lord is the beginning of wisdom." The word "fear" is a semantic oddity in the Bible. It means reverent mindfulness of God's infinite power and presence and total control over His creation. This is the beginning of right practice.

We have the illusion that we make the decision to meditate. This is not true. We are drawn toward meditation, drawn to God. Sometimes we are driven by suffering, but always the Christ is drawing us. We are drawn to Christhood, towards God, towards enlightenment. "If I be lifted up from the earth, I will draw all men unto me" (John 12:32).

MEDITATION ON THE LORD'S PRAYER

Our Father which art in heaven, Hallowed be thy name.

    1. I cherish the knowledge of God as omniactive Love-Intelligence.

Thy Kingdom come. Thy will be done, on earth, as it is in heaven.

    2. Heavenly harmony is available here and now to the "shouldless."

Give us this day our daily bread.

    3. The good of God is realized daily as inspired wisdom — peace, assurance, gratitude and love (PAGL).

And forgive us our debts, as we forgive our debtors.

    4. I abandon the error of interaction thinking.

And lead us not into temptation, but deliver us from evil:

    5. God-consciousness is immune to seduction, provocation and intimidation.

For thine is the kingdom, and the power, and the glory, forever.

6. God-centered living is the only alternative to self-confirmatory ideation.

THE FOUR W'S — A MEDITATION ON OUR IDENTITY

WHO AM I?

I am an image and likeness of God, a manifestation of Love-Intelligence.

WHAT AM I?

I am a divine consciousness.

WHERE AM I?

I live and move and have my being in omniactive divine Mind.

WHAT IS MY PURPOSE?

My purpose is to be a beneficial presence in the world.

THE PRAYER OF GLOWING

"Now is the accepted time..."
Now the Eye of my eyes is open
Now the Ear of my ears hears
Now the Mind of my mind knows
Now the Love of my love glows.
"I and my Father are one..."

TWO MEDITATIONS

Man is but a tear drop
Falling from the sky.
Time is but a moment;
Darkness lives to die.

Man is not a tear drop
Falling from above.
Joy is man,
And Love.

* * * * *

Living is strain
Dying is pain
Be still desire
Do not complain.

Suffering pleasure?
Enjoying pain?
Life's fading treasure
All seems in vain.

Not to resist
Neither give in
These are the source
Of suffering within.

Painless hurt
Joy 'stead of pleasure
Letting be
Is freedom's measure.

Serenely in Life
But guiding it not
Having desires
Yet desiring them not.

Loving existence
Yet clutching it not
Expecting death
Yet fearing it not.

Living is strain
Dying is pain
Be still desire
Do not complain.

— — — —

All suffering is vain.
Beyond the "I"
There is no one to pain
And no one to die.

This booklet is one of a series of twelve essays by Thomas Hora, M.D.

Healing Through Spiritual Understanding
A Hierarchy of Values
Forgiveness
The Soundless Music of Life
Can Meditation Be Done?
Marriage and Family Life
Compassion
God in Psychiatry
What Does God Want?
Self-Transcendence
Right Usefulness
Commentaries on Scripture

Other Books by Thomas Hora, M.D.

Beyond the Dream (New York: Crossroad, 1996)
Dialogues in Metapsychiatry (New York: Crossroad, 1996)
Existential Metapsychiatry (New York: Seabury Press, 1977)
In Quest of Wholeness

If you are interested in exploring more of Metapsychiatry's literature, please communicate with us at:

The PAGL Bookstore
P.O. Box 4001
Old Lyme, CT 06371
tel: 860-434-2999
email: PAGLBooks@aol.com
or visit Metapsychiatry's website: http://www.pagl.org

NOTES

NOTES

NOTES

NOTES

NOTES